LEARN TO DO
Hairpin Lace™

General Information

Many of the products used in this pattern book can be purchased from local craft, fabric and variety stores, or from the Annie's Attic Needlecraft Catalog (see Customer Service information on page 32).

Introduction

Hairpin lace is a decorative braid with a series of picot-like loops running along both edges. The loops are held in place by a rib which may be centered or offset. The rib is usually made of single crochet stitches but other stitches can be used for different effects.

The braid is made on a frame constructed of 2 or 3 parallel rods with the aid of a crochet hook.

Strips of braid may be used as they come off the frame as a trim. More often strips are combined into larger pieces by looping or crocheting them together or combining with crochet.

Originally, hairpin lace was made from fine threads on a large hairpin (*the open kind used for attaching hairpieces*). For wider braids or braids with an offset rib, the lace maker might have used a dinner fork or meat fork for the frame. Today commercial frames are used that are composed of 2 or 3 parallel rods held in position by a spacer at the

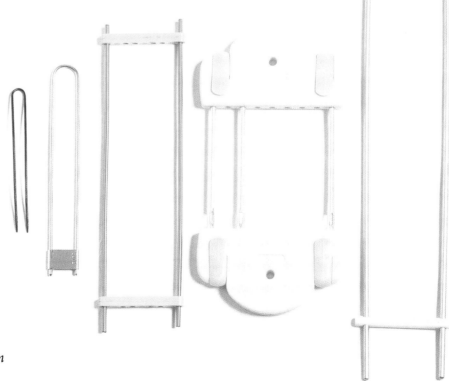

Photo A. Variety of hairpin frames. Left to right: ⅜ inch black enameled frame in form of hairpin without a spacer at the bottom, c. 1900; ¾ inch Boye frame, c. 1960; adjustable Susan Bates frame, c. 1970; adjustable Clover frame with 3 rods, 2003; 2 inch Boye frame, c. 1970

bottom and either a solid or removable spacer at the top. Some frames, especially older ones, are designed to produce only a single width of braid. Most modern frames are adjustable, so 1 frame will make a variety of widths. The Clover frame with 3 rods is needed to make hairpin lace with an offset rib.

YARNS & THREADS

Nearly any thread or yarn can be used to make hairpin lace. The key is to make the braid in a width that shows off your yarn to the best advantage. Here are some guidelines.

- Use fine, stiff threads for edgings on household linens. A thread with a tight twist, such as Red Heart Crochet Cotton, is ideal because the stiffness helps keep the loops in order and open.

- When using worsted weight yarn for afghans, keep the loops short so that the afghan doesn't become too open and lose its body. The afghan will be warmer and no one likes his or her toes sticking through the fabric.

- Fuzzy and novelty yarns worked on a large frame show off the yarn to best advantage.

- Mix yarns with varying textures, weights and colors in alternating strips for more interest.

- Combine multiple threads for fringes.

GAUGE

A hairpin lace strip is stretchy. You cannot accurately measure the gauge of a hairpin strip.

For trims and fringes that use the braid as it comes from the frame, work as much braid as you think you will need and then stretch to fit. For a thin trim or fringe, work less. For a thicker trim or fringe, work more. A swatch can give you a guideline as to how much braid to make.

If a braid is finished with crochet, the crochet determines the gauge of the piece.

THE BRAID STRIP

Every hairpin lace project starts by making the braid strip(s). The strip is formed by wrapping yarn around 1 rod of a frame creating a loop. Then the loop is locked into place by crocheting a stitch over the previous loop. There are many variations on how the yarn is wrapped and how the crochet stitch is formed. We have included instructions for the Basic Braid and several variations. For practice, we suggest you make a Basic Braid following the instructions below.

BASIC BRAID

Basic braid is formed by first wrapping yarn around a frame to form a loop. This is accomplished by turning the frame. Then the loop is locked it into place with one single crochet stitch worked into the front of previous loop. These stitches form the rib of the braid. The width of the braid and the size of the loops are determined by the width of the frame you choose or as indicated in the pattern (see photo B). The size of the rib is determined by the yarn size, hook size and stitch used.

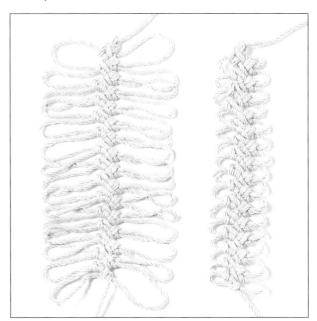

Photo B. Basic braids with loops of different sizes.

BASIC BRAID
INSTRUCTIONS

1. Position frame with spacer at bottom and rods 2½ inches apart. With yarn, make 1¼ inch loop with slip knot and place loop on left rod, having yarn end from skein in front of right rod. Bring yarn around right rod and across back of frame *(see illustration 1)*.

2. Insert hook through loop from bottom to top *(see illustration 2)*.

3. Hook yarn and pull through loop *(see illustration 3)*, ch 1 *(see illustration 4)*.

4. Drop loop from hook, with hook behind frame. Insert hook from back to front through loop just dropped, turn frame clockwise from right to left keeping yarn to back of frame *(loop forms around rod)*, insert hook under front strand of left loop *(see illustration 5)*, yo, pull through, yo and pull through 2 loops on hook *(see illustration 6, single crochet completed)*.

Rep step 4 for desired length of braid *(see illustration 7)*. Fasten off by cutting yarn and pull end through last loop on hook.

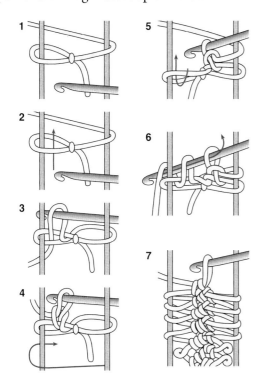

Try to keep the first few single crochet stitches of the rib centered between the rods. After you complete several loops, the single crochet stitches will keep themselves centered.

Many projects require hairpin strips with more loops than can fit on the frame. When the frame becomes full, count the loops on 1 rod and mark each 10th, 25th or 50th loop with a marker, such as split ring stitch markers or lengths of yarn. Slide the bottom spacer off of the frame and remove most of the loops. Add ribbon, thread, or yarn to the bottom of each rod and slip loops onto them to keep loops in order. Put the spacer back in place and continue making loops.

When additional yarn is needed, add the new yarn along the outside edge of a rod by tying the 2 strands of the old and new yarns together. After strips have been assembled, simply weave the ends through the crochet stitches used to join the strips. On some patterns, you may need to add yarn while crocheting the rib section in order to hide the ends.

BASIC BRAID VARIATIONS

There are many variations you can make to the basic braid. These variations change the look of the rib and change the spacing of the loops. Like basic braid, all create a rib with a zigzag pattern.

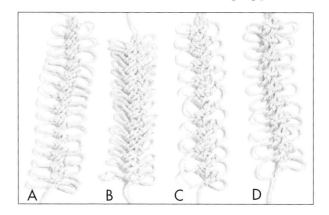

Photo C. Variations of basic braid: dc over front strand (A), basic sc over front and back strands (B), 2 sc over front strand (C), braid with sc over front strand (D).

BRAID WITH OTHER STITCHES OVER 1 OR BOTH STRANDS

Worked same as Basic Braid except with a double crochet over the front strand. Taller stitches such as double crochet and triple crochet space the loops farther apart. Two or more different stitches can be worked over a strand such as a single crochet and double crochet (*see A in Photo C on page 3*).

BASIC BRAID WITH SINGLE CROCHET WORKED OVER FRONT & BACK STRANDS

Worked same as Basic Braid except single crochet over both front and back strands of previous loop (*see B in Photo C on page 3*).

BASIC BRAID WITH MULTIPLE SINGLE CROCHET OVER 1 OR BOTH STRANDS

Worked same as Basic Braid except with 2 single crochet stitches over the front strand (*see C in Photo C on page 3*).

BASIC BRAID WITH SINGLE CROCHET WORKED OVER FRONT STRAND

Basic Braid with single crochet worked over front strand (*see D in Photo C on page 3*).

BRAID WITH CROCHET BETWEEN LOOPS

Wide braids can be made by working crochet between instead of over the loops. A variety of crochet stitches or simple patterns can be used. For example, a braid with 5 single crochet stitches between the loops is shown in Photo D. To make a sample of this braid, follow the instructions below.

Photo D. A braid with 5 single crochet stitches between loops.

SAMPLE BRAID INSTRUCTIONS

Row 1: Make loop with slip knot and place on left rod. Insert hook in loop from bottom to top, yo and pull through, ch 6, drop loop from hook, pass strand around right rod and across back, insert hook in loop in front of work.

Row 2: Sk first ch, sc in each of next 5 chs, ch 1, drop loop from hook, from back of frame insert hook in loop from back to front, turn frame clockwise.

Row 3: Sc in each of next 5 sc, ch 1, drop loop from hook, from back of frame insert hook in loop from back to front, turn frame clockwise.

Next rows: Rep row 3 for desired length.

BRAID FROM 2 YARNS 2-COLOR BRAID

Braids can also be made using 2 different colors of yarn (*see Photo E*). One yarn forms the loops which are wrapped around and around the frame without turning. The other yarn captures 1 or more strands as the rib is formed over the loops. The loops in these braids are not securely locked into place. A snag can distort a loop and its neighbors.

Any stitch that ends with a single centered loop can be used to form the rib in this type of braid. The simplest is a chain stitch. But stitches from the popcorn and cluster families can also be used.

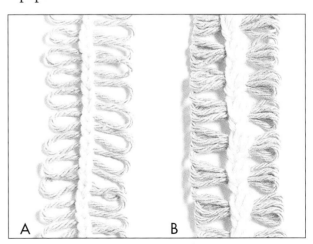

Photo E. Chain rib over single strand (A), cluster rib over groups of 3 loops (B).

CHAIN RIB

A in Photo E shows a chain rib over 1 strand.

Work as follows:

With first color yarn, make loop with slip knot and place loop over left rod. Wrap yarn around and around frame until desired number of loops are formed. With 2nd yarn, make loop with slip knot. Hold loop and yarn at back of frame. With hook, pull loop to front below first wrap, keeping yarn at back. Insert hook from front to back above one strand, yo and pull through loop on hook–chain stitch made, *insert hook above next strand, ch 1* rep between * until all strands are used.

CLUSTER RIB

Example in Photo E uses a cluster over groups of 3 loops (6 strands).

Work as follows:
With first color yarn, make loop with slip knot and place loop over left rod. Wrap yarn around and around frame until desired number of loops are in place. With 2nd yarn, make loop with slip knot.

For first cluster: Hold loop and yarn at back of frame, with hook, pull loop to front below first wrap, keeping yarn at back, [insert hook from front to back above 3 loops (6 strands), yo, pull to front, insert hook below loops, yo] twice, insert hook above 3 loops, yo and pull through all loops on hook, working loops off 1 or 2 at a time if necessary (cluster made), ch 1.

Remaining loops: [Insert hook above 3 loops (6 strands), yo, insert hook in ch 1, yo, pull through ch] twice, insert hook above same 3 loops, yo and pull through all loops on hook (cluster made), ch 1.

BRAID WITH OFFSET RIB

Braid with an offset rib is ideal for trims and fringes although it can be used in larger projects too. This braid is made with a Clover frame that has 3 rods. Two of the rods are placed close together and the 3rd farther away.

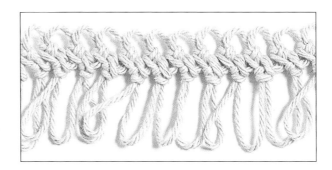

Photo F. Braid with offset rib.

INSTRUCTIONS

Hold frame with narrow space to left and wide space to right.

1. With yarn, make loop with slip knot and place loop over closest two rods of frame. Hold yarn at front. Wrap yarn counterclockwise around farthest rod and to back. In narrow space, pull up a loop under front strand, yo above strand, pull through (first loop made).

2. Drop loop from hook, from back of frame insert hook in loop from back to front, turn frame clockwise so yarn wraps around edge of frame with rods closest together (2nd loop made), in wide space, sc over front strand close to center rod.

3. Drop loop from hook, from back of frame insert hook in loop from back to front, turn frame clockwise so yarn wraps around edge of frame with rods farthest apart (3rd loop made), in narrow space, sc over front strand.

4. Rep steps 2 and 3 for desired length.

Many Basic Braid variations can be adapted to offset ribs such as working over both front and back strands and using stitches other than single crochet.

DECORATIVE TREATMENTS FOR LOOPS

Unless making a fringe, braid strips are either joined to each other or the edges are finished. While joining or edging, the loops themselves can be manipulated into decorative patterns. They may be open, twisted, grouped or crossed.

These decorative loops can be used with any of the joinings or edge finishes described later. The examples here use a single crochet edge.

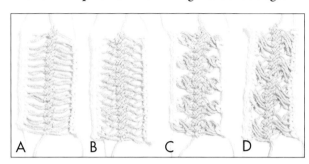

Photo G. Open loops (A), twisted loops (B), grouped loops with twist (C), crossed loops open (D)

OPEN LOOPS

Enter loop from front to back, yo, pull through loop, yo and pull through 2 loops on hook (*sc made*). Rep along edge of braid.

TWISTED LOOPS

Insert hook from back to front, bring hook to normal crochet position, yo, pull through loop, yo and pull through 2 loops on hook (*sc made*). Rep along braid.

GROUPED LOOPS

Open or twisted loops may be grouped together in groups of any number of loops. To group open loops together with an sc, insert hook through each loop from front to back, keeping each loop on hook, yo and pull through all but 2 loops on hook, yo and pull through 2 loops on hook (*sc made*). To keep braid flat, work 1, 2 or 3 chs between groups.

To group 3 twisted loops, as shown in Photo G, enter first loop from back to front, enter 2nd loop from back to front, enter 3rd loop from back to front, bring hook to normal crochet position, yo and pull through all 3 loops, yo and pull through 2 loops on hook (*sc made*). To keep braid flat, work 1, 2 or 3 chs between groups.

Loops may be grouped together with other stitches, such as double crochets or triple crochets.

To group 3 loops together with a dc, yo, insert hook in first loop, yo, pull through loop, yo and pull through 2 lps on hook, [yo, insert hook in next loop, yo, pull through loop, yo and pull through 2 lps on hook] twice, yo and pull through all 3 lps on hook (*dc made*).

CROSSED LOOPS

For 2-over-2 crossed loops with the loops worked open as shown in Photo G, sk 2 loops, enter 3rd loop from front to back, yo and pull through loop, yo and pull through 2 loops on hook (*sc made*), enter 4th loop from front to back, yo and pull through loop, yo and pull through 2 loops on hook (*sc made*), enter first skipped loop from front to back, yo and pull through loop, yo and pull through 2 loops on hook (*sc made*), enter 2nd skipped loop from front to back, yo and pull through loop, yo and pull through 2 loops on hook (*sc made*).

Repeat with groups of 4 loops along edge of braid.

EDGES

Edges are used to stabilize and/or finish edges of braid strips. Edges may be made without adding yarn by chaining loops together. Or they may be made by working crochet stitches through the loops.

LOOPED EDGE

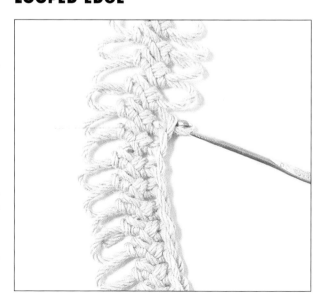

Photo H. Looped edge.

LOOPED EDGE

Insert hook in first loop, *insert hook in next loop, pull loop through loop on hook*, repeat between * for desired length. Secure last loop by tying end of rib through loop.

SINGLE CROCHET EDGE

Single crochet is the simplest and fastest way to edge a braid strip. For braids with single crochet ribs, one single crochet stitch in each loop is used. For braids using taller stitches, like double crochet which spread the loops apart, or for grouped loops, single crochet stitches are spaced with chain stitches.

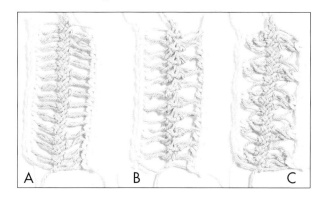

Photo I. Single crochet in each loop on braid with single crochet rib (A), (single crochet, chain 1) on braid with double crochet rib (B), (single crochet in 3 loops, chain 2 or 3) on braid with grouped loops (C).

SINGLE CROCHET EDGE ON BRAID WITH SINGLE CROCET RIB

Sc in each loop along edge.

SINGLE CROCHET EDGE ON BRAID WITH DOUBLE CROCHET RIB

Sc in loop, ch 1, rep between * along edge.

SINGLE CROCHET EDGE ON GROUPED LOOPS

*Sc dec *(see Stitch Guide)* in next 3 loops, ch 2 or ch 3 so that braid lies flat*, rep between * along edge.

EDGES USING OTHER CROCHET STITCHES

Edges using double crochet and taller stitches make a more flexible braid than single crochet. The loops are not held as rigidly in place allowing the braid to flex more easily. This type of edge is often used in laces where the braid forms a serpentine shape. Combine this type of edge with a narrow rib which also makes a braid more flexible.

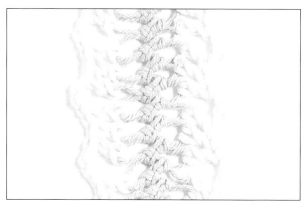

Photo J. Braid edged with double crochet and chain stitches.

BRAID WITH DOUBLE CROCHET EDGE

Photo J shows sample that combines double crochet and chain stitches.

Dc in each of next 3 loops, ch 3, rep between * along edge.

BRAID JOININGS

Braid strips can be joined together to form larger pieces. Joinings are made with the loops. The 2 most common methods of joining strips are looping and crocheting.

LOOPED JOINING

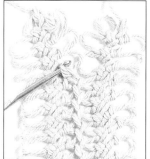 

Photo K. Left to right: looped join, looped join using groups of 2 loops.

A Looped Joining joins 2 strips of hairpin lace without using any additional yarn. The loops can be joined singly or in groups. The joining process can be done with either a crochet hook or the fingers depending on the size of loops.

LOOPED JOINING WITH SINGLE LOOPS

Lay 2 lengths of braid next to each other lining up loops, insert hook in first loop of right braid, insert hook in first loop of left braid, *pull loop of left braid through, insert hook in next loop of right braid, pull loop through, insert hook in next loop of left braid*, repeat between * for length of braid, alternating left loop and right loop. Secure last loop by tying yarn end of rib through loop.

LOOPED JOINING USING GROUPS OF LOOPS

For groups of 2 loops as shown in Photo K on page 7, lay 2 lengths of braid next to each other lining up loops, insert hook in first 2 loops of right braid, insert hook in first 2 loops of left braid, *pull loops of left braid through, insert hook in next 2 loops of right braid, pull loops through, insert hook in next 2 loops of left braid*, repeat between * for length of braid, alternating 2 left loops and 2 right loops. Secure last loop by tying yarn end of rib through loop.

SINGLE CROCHET JOINING

Single crochet can be used to join braid strips loop-to-loop or to join a braid strip to a crocheted piece (sometimes referred to as a crochet ground). In general, hold the 2 pieces to be joined with wrong sides together and single crochet through corresponding loops of both pieces or through corresponding loop and stitch of both pieces. If the 2 pieces do not line up stitch for stitch, work some single crochets through 1 side only or group some loops together to keep pieces even.

EDGED BRAIDS JOINED LOOP-TO-LOOP

Hold strips wrong sides together, matching loops, sc though 1 loop from front braid and 1 loop from back together at same time, repeat for length of braid.

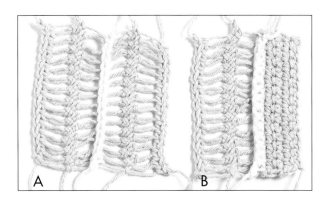

Photo L. Two braid strips joined loop-to-loop (A), braid strip joined to single crochet ground (B).

EDGED BRAID JOINED TO CROCHET PIECE

Hold strip and crochet piece with wrong sides together, matching loops with stitches in piece, sc 1 loop and 1 stitch of piece together at same time, repeat for length of braid.

JOIN EDGED BRAIDS

Strips are often edged and then the edged strips joined. A row of single crochet for the first row of an edging gives maximum stability. Then more rows in various stitches can be added to provide a decorative effect. The additional rows of stitches typically use stitch combinations that are used as edgings on crochet such as a fan stitch edge or row(s) of double crochet. The edged braids are then joined just as crochet pieces are joined. The single crochet join and the chain mesh join are favorites.

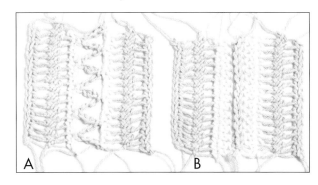

Photo M. Braid edged with single crochet and then strips joined with chain mesh (A), braid edged with a row of single crochet, and then a row of double crochet and joined with single crochet (B).

CHAIN MESH JOINING FOR EDGED BRAIDS

Example in Photo M uses braid strips edged in single crochet.

Hold braid strips with wrong sides together, carefully matching loops, sl st in first sc in edge of front braid, sl st in 2nd sc on back braid, *sk next 2 sc in front braid, sl st in next sc, sk next 2 sc on back braid, sl st in next sc*, repeat between * for length of braids.

SINGLE CROCHET JOINING FOR EDGED BRAIDS

Example in Photo M uses braid strips edged in single crochet.

Hold braid strips with wrong sides together, carefully matching loops, sc through both lps of each sc of front and back braids together at same time, repeat for length of braids.

RIB JOINING

A single braid strip may be joined to form a ring. To do this, join the ends of the rib using the yarn ends of the rib and a crochet hook or tapestry needle. Insert the ends through the rib completing the rib pattern as much as possible. Finish off on the wrong side.

ROSETTES

Braid strips can also be formed into circles or squares for use in motifs. The loops are gathered together on one side to form a center. The loops on the outer side are worked or in groups. Loops can be worked either open or twisted. The braid strip needs to be flexible to form a circle or square so use a narrow rib such as single crochet or chain and long loops.

Photo N. Round rosette with tied center and twisted loops.

Photo O. Square rosette with single crochet edge for center and open loops.

CIRLCE ROSETTE WITH TIED CENTER & TWISTED LOOPS

Photo N uses 24 loops on each side of braid strip.

Before removing strip from frame, pass a 1 inch length of yarn through all loops on 1 side. Remove braid from frame. Tie ends of 1 inch length together so a small hole forms in center of rosette. Join rib using yarn tails of rib and a crochet hook or tapestry needle. Insert the tails through the rib completing the rib pattern as much as possible. Finish off on wrong side. Around outer edge, sc in each loop, inserting hook from back to front to twist loops. Make 2 chs between each sc. Join to form a ring.

SQUARE ROSETTE WITH SINGLE CROCHET EDGE FOR CENTER & OPEN LOOPS

Photo O uses 32 loops on each side of braid strip.

Along 1 edge of braid strip, [sc dec (see Stitch Guide) in next 4 loops] 8 times, inserting hook from front to back to keep loops open, join to form ring. Join rib using yarn tails of rib and a crochet hook or tapestry needle. Insert the tails through the rib completing the rib pattern as much as possible. Finish off on back. Working around outer edge, *tr dec (see Stitch Guide) in next 4 loops (corner made), ch 5, [sc dec in next 2 loops, ch 5] twice*, rep between * around rosette. Join to form square. ∎

Cozy Cold Weather Scarf

DESIGN BY **NANCY NEHRING**

SKILL LEVEL

BEGINNER

FINISHED SIZE
5 x 54 inches, excluding fringe

MATERIALS
- Medium (worsted) weight yarn: 36 oz/1,800 yds/1,020g orange variegated
- Size J/10/6mm crochet hook
- Clover tool set at 6 and 8 or 3-inch hairpin frame
- 4 large safety pins

4 MEDIUM

GAUGE
Gauge is not important for this item.

INSTRUCTIONS
BRAID STRIPS
MAKE 3.

1. Position frame with spacer at bottom and rods 2½ inches apart. With 3 strands of yarn, make 1¼ inch loop with slip knot and place loop on left rod, having yarn end from skein in front of right rod. Bring yarn around right rod and across back of frame (*see illustration 1*).

2. Insert hook through loop from bottom to top (*see illustration 2*).

3. Hook yarn and pull through loop (*see illustration 3*), ch 1 (*see illustration 4*).

4. Drop loop from hook, with hook behind frame. Insert hook from back to front through loop just dropped, turn frame clockwise from right to left keeping yarn to back of frame (*loop forms around rod*), insert hook under front strand of left loop (*see illustration 5*), yo, pull through, yo and pull through 2 loops on hook (*see illustration 6 single crochet completed*).

5. Rep step 4 making 100 loops on each side (*see illustration 7*). Leaving 8-inch end, fasten off by cutting yarn and pull end through last loop on hook.

ASSEMBLY
Lay 2 Braid Strips next to each other with beg ends at same end.

Looped Joining joins 2 strips of hairpin lace without using any additional yarn. The loops can be joined individually or in groups (*see Photo K on page 7*). The joining

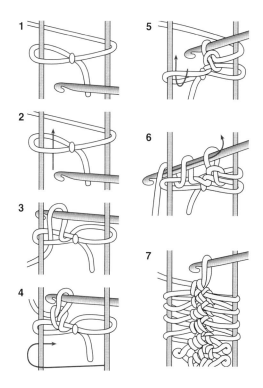

process can be done with either a crochet hook or the fingers depending on the size of loops. Do not secure end loops. Place safety pin through last 2 loops.

Join 3rd Braid in same manner.

FINISHING
Insert hook in first loop, *insert hook in next loop, pull loop through loop on hook*, rep between * around outer edge of assembled piece. Do not secure last loop. Place large safety pin through last 2 loops.

FRINGE
Cut 12-inch strands of yarn. Holding 3 strands tog, fold in half, pull fold through, pull ends through fold. Pull to tighten.

Fringe in loops marked with safety pins and in rem loops at short ends of Braid. Trim ends. ∎

Cozy Cold Weather Hat

DESIGN BY **NANCY NEHRING**

SKILL LEVEL

INTERMEDIATE

FINISHED SIZES
Instructions for adult size small; changes for medium and large sizes are in [ ].

MATERIALS
- Medium (worsted) weight yarn: 4 oz/200 yds/113g orange variegated
- Size H/8/5mm crochet hook or size needed to obtain gauge
- Clover tool set at 6 and 8 or 3-inch hairpin frame
- Tapestry needle
- 4 large safety pins
- Straight pins

4 MEDIUM

GAUGE
Rib pattern: 5 sl sts = 1 inch; 7 rows = 1 inch

INSTRUCTIONS
BRAID STRIPS
FIRST BRAID STRIP
1. Position frame with spacer at bottom and rods 2½ inches apart. With 2 strands of yarn, make 1¼ inch loop with slip knot and place loop on left rod, having yarn end from skein in front of right rod. Bring yarn around right rod and across back of frame (*see illustration 1*).

2. Insert hook through loop from bottom to top (*see illustration 2*).

3. Hook yarn and pull through loop (*see illustration 3*), ch 1 (*see illustration 4*).

4. Drop loop from hook, with hook behind frame. Insert hook from back to front through loop just dropped, turn frame clockwise from right to left keeping yarn to back of frame (*loop forms around rod*), insert hook under front strand of left loop (*see illustration 5*), yo, pull through, yo and pull through 2 loops on hook (*see illustration 6 single crochet completed*).

5. Rep step 4 making 50 loops on each side (*see illustration 7*) on each side. Leaving 8-inch end, fasten off by cutting yarn and pulling end through last loop on hook.

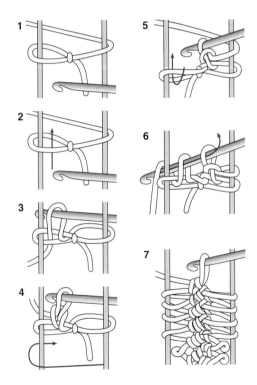

2ND BRAID STRIP

Rep First Braid Strip making 25 loops on each side, but do not remove from frame.

CROWN

1. Form 2nd Braid Strip into rosette by tying center loops tog and joining ends of rib tog.

2. Before removing strip from frame, pass a 1-inch length of yarn through all loops on 1 side. Remove braid from frame. Tie ends of

1-inch length together so a small hole forms in center of rosette. Join rib using yarn tails of rib and a crochet hook or tapestry needle. Insert the tails through the rib completing the rib pattern as much as possible.

3. Join ends of rib on First Braid in same manner.

4. Insert hook in 2 loops of First Braid, insert hook in 1 loop of 2nd Braid, *pull loops through, insert hook in next 2 loops of First Braid, pull loops through, insert hook in next loop on 2nd Braid*, rep between * around, wrap last loop(s) around post of first loop(s) and secure with yarn end from rib.

LOOPED EDGE

Insert hook in first loop, *insert hook in next loop, pull loop through loop on hook*, rep between * around, wrap last loop around post of first loop and secure with yarn end from rib.

BRIM

Row 1: Ch 17 [21, 25], working in **back lps** (*see Stitch Guide*), sl st in 2nd ch from hook and in each ch across, turn.

Row 2: Working in back lps, ch 1, sl st in each st across, turn.

Rows 3–132: Rep row 2. At end of last row, leaving long end, fasten off.

ASSEMBLY

Sew row 1 and row 132 of Brim tog.

Pin Brim to bottom edge of Crown. With RS of Brim facing, join with sc in sp between ribs on Brim and in corresponding front loop (*both strands*) of looped Edge on Crown, working through both pieces at same time and working around Brim, sc in sp between each rib on Brim and in corresponding front loop (*both strands*) of Crown edge, working 2 sc in same loops of Looped Edge is necessary, join with sl st in beg sc.

POMPOM

Cut 12-inch length of yarn. Set aside. Wrap yarn 100 times around frame. Tie 12-inch strand tightly around center of wraps. Cut wraps apart along rods. Trim Pompom into ball. Tie Pompom to center top of Hat. ∎

Ribbon-Candy Afghan

DESIGN BY **NANCY NEHRING**

SKILL LEVEL

INTERMEDIATE

FINISHED SIZE
44 x 74 inches

MATERIALS
- Medium (worsted) weight yarn:
    36 oz/1,800 yds/1,020g white
    6 oz/300 yds/170g each lime, pink, orange, yellow, lavender and turquoise
- Sizes H/8/5mm and J/10/6mm crochet hooks or size needed to obtain gauge
- Clover tool set at 6 and 8 or 3-inch hairpin frame

GAUGE
Size J hook: 19 sc = 8 inches

INSTRUCTIONS
CHAIN RIB BRAID STRIPS
MAKE 3 IN TURQUOISE AND 2 EACH IN LIME, PINK, ORANGE, YELLOW AND LAVENDER.

Cut 3 strands 15 yds long of each of other colors.

With 1 strand white and 1 stand 2nd color held tog, with size H hook, make lp with slip knot and place lp over left rod. Wrap yarn around and around frame until desired number of lps are formed. With 2nd yarn, make lp with slip knot. Hold lp and yarn at back of frame. With hook, pull lp to front below first wrap, keeping yarn at back. Insert hook from front to back above 1 strand, yo and pull through lp on hook *(ch made)*, *insert hook above next strand, ch 1*, rep between * until all strands are used and you have 175 lps on each side. End by pulling end of yarn used for ch st through last ch. Tie end to 2 yarns used to form lps.

EDGING

Work all lps open. Hold strip with 1 side of lps at top, hold first lp at right-hand edge open with right side of ch at base facing; with white and size J hook, make slip knot on hook, remove lp from hook and hold in back of open lp, insert hook in open lp from front to back, twist lp by bringing head of hook to right of lp around front and back to beg position with head of hook pointing toward back of work, twist lp in same manner once more, insert hook in lp made by slip knot and draw through twisted lp.

Row 1: Ch 1, *insert hook in next open lp, twist twice, yo, pull lp through, yo and pull through 2 lps on hook, rep from * across. Turn.

Row 2: Ch 1, sc in each st and beg ch-1. Fasten off.

Work Edging in same manner on other lp side.

ASSEMBLY

Arrange Braid Strips in following color sequence: turquoise, lavender, pink, yellow, orange, lime, turquoise, lime, orange, yellow, pink, lavender and turquoise.

To join braid strips, hold 2 Braid Strips with WS tog, with size J hook and white, make slip knot on hook, remove lp from hook and pass hook through first sc of both braids, pull lp through, working through both thicknesses at same time, [ch 1, sl st in next sc] across braid. Fasten off.

Join rem Braid Strips in same manner.

EDGING

Hold Afghan with 1 short end at top, join white in first st in upper right-hand corner, ch 1, *4 sc in next twisted lp, sk next rib, 4 sc in next twisted lp, sc in row 1 of white edge, sk next joining, sc in row 1 of next white edge, rep from * across. Fasten off.

Rep on rem short end. At end of Edging, **do not fasten off**.

BORDER

Working across next side, sc in each st to first sc of Edging, 3 sc in first sc of Edging, working across Edging, sc in each sc to last sc, 3 sc in last sc, working across next side, sc in each st to first sc of Edging, 3 sc in first sc, working across Edging, sc in each sc to last sc, 3 sc in last sc, join with sl st in beg sc. Fasten off.

FINISHING

Steam Afghan to relax yarn and reset twist in lps. Set iron on synthetic and maximum steam. Working in small areas, hold iron several inches above Afghan, stretching braid widthwise so twisted lps lie flat. Steam heavily and let cool. ■

Fun-Loving Afghan

DESIGN BY **NANCY NEHRING**

SKILL LEVEL

INTERMEDIATE

FINISHED SIZE
42 x 57 inches

MATERIALS
- Medium (worsted) weight yarn:
  - 17 oz/850 yds/482g variegated
  - 14 oz/700 yds/397g each red, purple, orange and yellow
- Size H/8/5mm crochet hook or size needed to obtain gauge
- Clover tool set at 4 and 6 or 2-inch hairpin frame

4 MEDIUM

GAUGE
3 dc = 1 inch

PATTERN NOTES
Chain-2 at beginning of row or round counts as first double crochet unless otherwise stated.

When joining Braid Strips to Afghan, loop refers to Braid loop and lp refers to lp on hook.

SPECIAL STITCH
Decrease (dec): Holding back last lp of each st on hook, dc in next ch, sk next ch, dc in next ch, yo, pull through all lps on hook.

BRAID STRIPS
MAKE 12.

1. Position frame with spacer at bottom and rods 2½ inches apart. With variegated, make 1¼-inch loop with slip knot and place loop on left rod, having yarn end from skein in front of right rod. Bring yarn around right rod and across back of frame *(see illustration 1)*.

2. Insert hook through loop from bottom to top *(see illustration 2)*.

3. Hook yarn and pull through loop *(see illustration 3)*, ch 1 *(see illustration 4)*.

4. Drop loop from hook, with hook behind frame. Insert hook from back to front through loop just dropped, turn frame clockwise from right to left keeping yarn to back of frame *(loop forms around rod)*, insert hook under front strand of left loop *(see illustration 5)*, yo, pull through, yo and pull through 2 loops on hook *(see illustration 6; single crochet completed)*.

Rep step 4, making 162 loops on each side *(see illustration 7)*. Fasten off by cutting yarn and pull end through last loop on hook. Set aside.

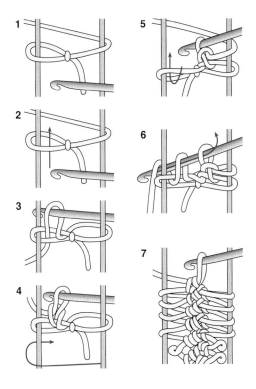

INSTRUCTIONS
AFGHAN

Row 1 (RS): With red, ch 146, dc in 4th ch from hook *(first 3 chs count as first dc)*, dc in each of next 9 chs, *(dc, ch 1, dc) in next ch, dc in each of next 10 chs**, **dec** *(see Special Stitch)*, rep from * across, ending last rep at **, sk next ch, dc in last ch, **changing colors** *(see Stitch Guide)* in last st to purple. Fasten off red.

Row 2: Ch 2 *(see Pattern Notes)*, sk next st, *dc in each of next 10 sts, (dc, ch 1, dc) in next ch sp, dc in each of next 10 sts**, dec, rep from * across, ending last rep at **, sk next st, dc in last st, changing to orange in last st, turn. Fasten off purple.

Row 3: Ch 2, sk next st, *dc in each of next 10 sts, (dc, ch 1, dc) in next ch sp, dc in each of next 10 sts**, dec, rep from * across, ending last rep at **, sk next st, dc in last st, changing to yellow, turn. Fasten off orange.

Row 4: Ch 2, sk next st, *dc in each of next 10 sts, 3 dc in next ch sp, dc in each of next 10 sts**, dec, rep from * across, ending last rep at **, sk next st, dc in last st, **do not** change colors, turn.

Row 5: Ch 1, sc in each of first 3 dc, hold 1 Braid Strip behind piece with top edge of the Braid Strip even with top edge of last row; ◊drop lp from hook, insert hook from back and from left to right through 3rd, 2nd, first loops on braid, keeping twist in loops, bring hook to normal crocheting position, with yarn in front of loops and taking care to keep normal size of dropped lp, yo close to dropped lp and pull through 3 loops on hook, insert hook from right to left through dropped lp and pull dropped lp through lp on hook, sc in next 3 dc◊, rep between ◊ twice,*[drop lp from hook, insert hook from back and from left to right through next 9 loops from 9th to first loops, keeping twist in loops, bring hook to normal crocheting position, with yarn in front of 9 loops, yo and through 9 loops, insert hook from right to left through dropped lp and pull dropped lp through lp on hook, sc in each of next 3 dc*; rep between ◊ 3 times, sc in each of next 2 dc,

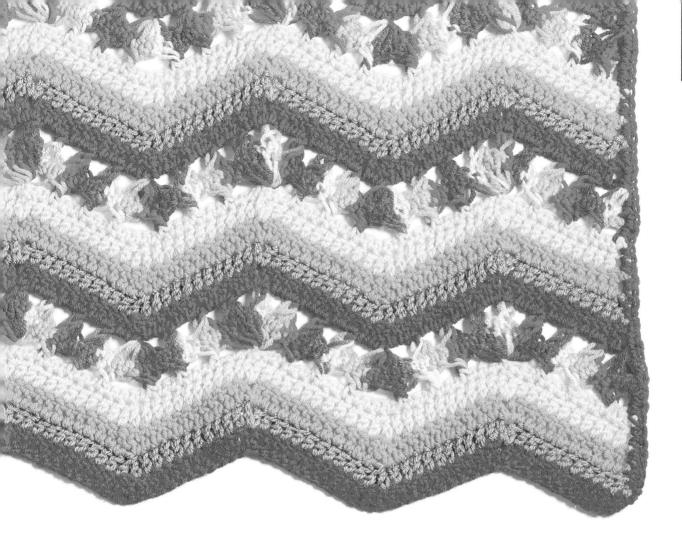

rep between ◊ 3 times] 5 times, and then rep between * once, rep between ◊ twice, drop lp from hook, insert hook from back and from left to right through 3rd, 2nd, first loops on braid, keeping twist in loops, bring hook to normal crocheting position, with yarn in front of loops and taking care to keep normal size of dropped lp, yo close to dropped lp and pull through 3 loops on hook, insert hook from right to left through dropped lp and pull dropped lp through lp on hook, sc in each of last 3 sts. Fasten off.

Unfold hairpin strip from behind work.

Row 6: Insert hook through braid loops from right to left, maintaining twist, hold piece with WS facing, join red with sl st in first sc of row 5, ch 2, sl st through end of rib on Braid Strip, ch 2, working across Braid Strip, [sc dec *(see Stitch Guide)* in next 3 loops, ch 2] 8 times, *sc dec in next 6 loops, ch 2, [sc dec in next 3 loops, ch 2] 7 times, rep from * 4 times, sc dec in next 6 loops, [ch 2, sc dec in next 3 loops] 7 times, ch 2, insert hook through last 3 loops, yo twice, pull up lp in end of rib, yo twice, insert hook in 2nd ch of turning ch of row 5, yo and pull lp through, [yo, pull through 2 lps on hook] 6 times, turn.

Row 7: Chs count as sts on this row, sk first st and next ch, *dc in each of next 10 sts, (dc, ch 1, dc) in next sc, dc in each of next 10 sts** dec, rep from * across, ending last rep at **, sk next 2 sts, dc in last st, changing to purple. Fasten off red.

Next rows: [Rep rows 2–7 consecutively] 11 times.

Next rows: [Rep rows 2–4] once. At end of last row, fasten off.

FINISHING

Hold Afghan with RS facing and 1 long edge at top, join red with sc in end of first row in upper corner, sc across side to corner, working 1 sc in end of each row and 3 sc in sps at end of Braid Strips and in ends of dc rows. Fasten off.

Rep on rem long side. ∎

Rosette Doily

DESIGN BY **NANCY NEHRING**

SKILL LEVEL

INTERMEDIATE

FINISHED SIZE
11 x 16½ inches

MATERIALS
- Size 10 crochet cotton:
  300 yds natural
- Size 7/1.65mm steel crochet hook or
  size needed to obtain gauge
- Clover tool set at center and 2 or
  ¾-inch hairpin frame
- Tapestry needle

GAUGE
Motif = 3 inches

PATTERN NOTE
Join with slip stitch as indicated unless
  otherwise stated.

SPECIAL STITCH
Cluster (cl): Holding back last lp of each
  st on hook, 3 dc in place indicated, yo,
  pull through all lps on hook.

INSTRUCTIONS
ROSETTE
MAKE 16
1. Position frame with spacer at bottom and
   rods 2½ inches apart. With yarn, make
   1¼-inch loop with slip knot and place loop
   on left rod, having yarn end from skein
   in front of right rod. Bring yarn around
   right rod and across back of frame
   (see illustration 1).

2. Insert hook through loop from bottom
   to top *(see illustration 2)*.

3. Hook yarn and pull through loop
   (see illustration 3), ch 1 *(see illustration 4)*.

4. Drop loop from hook, with hook behind
   frame. Insert hook from back to front
   through loop just dropped, turn frame
   clockwise from right to left keeping yarn to
   back of frame *(loop forms around rod)*, insert
   hook under front strand of left loop *(see
   illustration 5)*, yo, pull through, yo and pull
   through 2 loops on hook *(see illustration
   6 single crochet completed)*.

Rep step 4 with 24 loops on each side
  (see illustration 7).

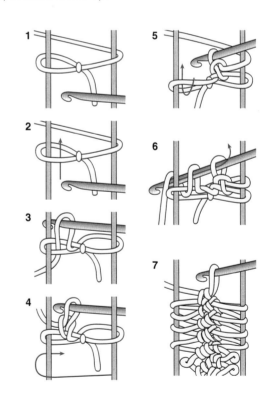

Pass 6-inch length of thread through all loops
  on 1 side and tie knot.

Join the ends of the rib using the yarn ends of the
  rib and a crochet hook or tapestry needle. Insert
  the ends through the rib completing the rib
  pattern as much as possible. Fasten off on WS.

DOILY
MOTIF
MAKE 16.

Rnd 1: Work all loops twisted by inserting hook from back to front through each loop, **join** *(see Pattern Note)* in any loop on 1 Rosette, **sc dec** *(see Stitch Guide)* in same loop and next 2 loops, ch 5, [sc dec in next 3 loops, ch 5] 7 times, join in beg sc.

Rnd 2: Ch 1, sc in first sc, 8 sc in next ch-5 sp, [sc in next sc, 8 sc in next ch-5 sp] 7 times, join in beg sc. *(73 sc)*

Rnd 3: Ch 1, sc in each of first 5 sc, *[ch 2, sk next sc, sc in next sc] 5 times**, sc in each of next 8 sc, rep from * around, ending last rep at **, sc in each of next 3 sc, join in beg sc.

Rnd 4: Ch 1, sc in each of first 4 sc, *sc in next ch-2 sp, ch 2, [cl *(see Special Stitch)* in next ch-2 sp, ch 2] 3 times**, sc in next ch-2 sp, sc in each of next 9 sc, rep from * around, ending last rep at **, sc in next ch-2 sp, sc in each of last 4 sc, join in beg sc.

Rnd 5: Ch 1, sc in same sc and in next 5 sc, *sc in next ch-2 sp, ch 3, [cl in next ch-2 sp, ch 3] twice**, sc in next ch-2 sp, sc in each of next 11 sc, rep from * around, ending last rep at **, sc in next ch-2 sp, sc in each of last 5 sc, join in beg sc.

Rnd 6: Ch 1, sc in each of first 7 sc, *sc in next ch-3 sp, ch 4, cl in next ch-3 sp, ch 4**, sc in next ch-3 sp, sc in each of next 13 sc, rep from * around, ending last rep at **, sc in next ch-3 sp, sc in each of last 6 sc, join in beg sc. Fasten off.

If Rosette causes completed square to pucker, loosen center of Rosette to create a larger center hole.

ASSEMBLY
With tapestry needle, sew Motifs tog in 4 rows of 4 Motifs each.

BORDER
Rnd 1: Hold piece with RS facing and 1 short edge at top, join in cl in upper right-hand corner, ch 1, 3 sc in same cl *(corner)*, *evenly sp 97 sc across to next outer cl, 3 sc in next cl *(corner)*, rep from * twice, sc in each sc and in each ch across to first sc, join in beg sc.

Rnd 2: Sl st in next sc, ch 3 *(counts as first dc)*, 8 dc in same sc *(corner)*, *sk next sc, [sc in next sc, sk next sc, 7 dc in next sc, sk next sc] 6 times, [sc in next sc, sk next 2 sc, 7 dc in next sc, sk next 2 sc] 8 times, [sc in next sc, sk next sc, 7 dc in next sc, sk next sc] 6 times, sc in next sc, sk next sc**, 9 dc in next sc *(corner)*, rep from * around, ending last rep at **, join in 3rd ch of beg ch-3. Fasten off. ■

Scalloped Lace Edging

DESIGN BY **NANCY NEHRING**

SKILL LEVEL

INTERMEDIATE

FINISHED SIZE
2½ inches wide by desired length

MATERIALS
- Size 10 crochet cotton:
    14 yds light green for each repeat
- Size 7/1.65mm steel crochet hook or size needed to obtain gauge
- Clover tool set at 2 and 4 or 1½-inch hairpin frame
- Tapestry needle

GAUGE
35 sts on rnd 2 of Header = 4 inches

Each repeat = 3 inches long

PATTERN NOTE
A standard pillowcase requires a basic braid of about 14 scallops or 448 loops.

Join with slip stitch as indicated unless otherwise stated.

INSTRUCTIONS
BRAID STRIP
1. Position frame with spacer at bottom and rods 2½ inches apart. Make 1¼ inch loop with slip knot and place loop on left rod, having yarn end from skein in front of right rod. Bring yarn around right rod and across back of frame (*see illustration 1*).

2. Insert hook through loop from bottom to top (*see illustration 2*).

3. Hook yarn and pull through loop (*see illustration 3*), ch 1 (*see illustration 4*).

4. Drop loop from hook, with hook behind frame. Insert hook from back to front through loop just dropped, turn frame clockwise from right to left keeping yarn to back of frame (*loop forms around rod*), insert hook under front strand of left loop (*see illustration 5*), yo, pull through, yo and pull through 2 loops on hook (*see illustration 6 single crochet completed*).

Rep step 4 making 32 loops on each side (*see illustration 7*). Fasten off by cutting yarn and pulling end through last loop on hook.

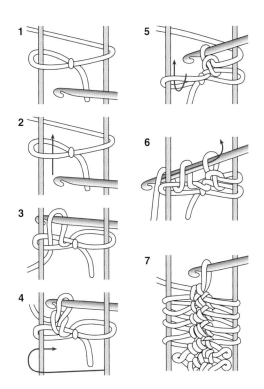

HEADER

Rnd 1: Hold braid with 1 side of loops at top, **join** (*see Pattern Notes*) in first loop at right-hand end of braid, **sc dec** (*see Stitch Guide*) in first 3 loops, [ch 3, sc in next loop] twice, ch 3, [sc dec in next 5 loops] 5 times, [ch 3, sc in next loop] twice, ch 3, *sc dec in next 3 loops, [ch 3, sc in next loop] twice, ch 3, [sc dec in next 5 loops] 5 times, [ch 3, sc in next loop] twice, ch 3, rep from * around, join in beg sc.

Rnd 2: Ch 1, *5 sc in next ch-3 sp, (2 hdc, 3 dc) in next ch-3 sp work (tr, 2 dtr) in next ch-3 sp, ch 1, (2 dtr, tr) in next ch-3 sp, (3 dc, 2 hdc) in next ch-3 sp, 5 sc in next ch-3 sp, rep from * around, join in beg sc. Fasten off.

LOWER EDGE

On following rnd, sc loops together, working all loops twisted by inserting hook from back to front through each loop.

Hold piece with Header at bottom (*see photo below*), join in loop above loop indicated by arrow in photo.

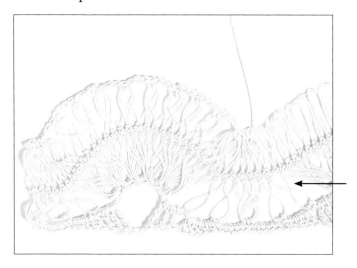

Rnd 1: Sc dec in same loop and next 5 loops, sc dec in next 5 loops, [ch 3, sc dec in next 2 loops] 8 times, ch 3, sc dec in next 5 loops, *sc dec in next 6 loops, sc dec in next 5 loops, [ch 3, sc dec in next 2 loops] 8 times, ch 3, sc dec in 5 loops, rep from * around, join in beg sc.

Rnd 2: Ch 1, *3 sc in next ch-3 sp, ch 3, sl st in first ch (picot), rep from * around, join in beg sc. Fasten off.

FINISHING

Join the ends of the rib using the yarn ends of the rib and a crochet hook or tapestry needle. Insert the ends through the rib completing the rib pattern as much as possible. Fasten off on the wrong side. ∎

Serpentine Lace Edging

DESIGN BY **NANCY NEHRING**

SKILL LEVEL

INTERMEDIATE

FINISHED SIZE

4 inches wide by desired length

MATERIALS

- Size 10 crochet cotton:
  16 yds light blue for each repeat
- Size 7/1.65mm steel crochet hook or size needed to obtain gauge
- Clover tool set at center and 2 or ¾-inch hairpin frame
- Tapestry needle

GAUGE

8 sc on rnd 3 of Header = 1 inch

Each repeat = 2 inches long

PATTERN NOTES

A standard pillowcase requires a basic braid of about 16 scallops or 640 loops.

Join with slip stitch as indicated unless otherwise stated.

INSTRUCTIONS

BRAID STRIP

1. Position frame with spacer at bottom and rods 2½ inches apart. With variegated, make 1¼ inch loop with slip knot and place loop on left rod, having yarn end from skein in front of right rod. Bring yarn around right rod and across back of frame (*see illustration 1*).

2. Insert hook through loop from bottom to top *(see illustration 2)*.

3. Hook yarn and pull through loop *(see illustration 3)*, ch 1 *(see illustration 4)*.

4. Drop loop from hook, with hook behind frame. Insert hook from back to front through loop just dropped, turn frame clockwise from right to left keeping yarn to back of frame *(loop forms around rod)*, insert hook under front strand of left loop *(see illustration 5)*, yo, pull through, yo and pull through 2 loops on hook *(see illustration 6 single crochet completed)*.

Rep step 4 making 32 loops on each side *(see illustration 7)*. Fasten off by cutting yarn and pulling end through last loop on hook.

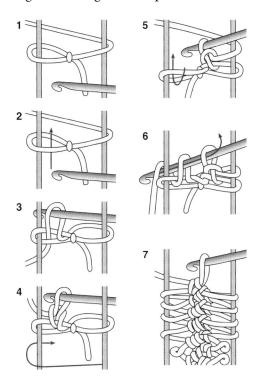

HEADER

Rnd 1: Hold braid with 1 side of loops at top, **join** *(see Pattern Notes)* in first loop at right-hand end of braid, ch 6 *(counts as first dc and ch-3)*, dc in next loop, [ch 3, dc in next loop] 3 times, *[ch 3, dc in each of next 3 loops] 3 times, ch 3, **dc dec** *(see Stitch Guide)* in next 3 loops, [dc dec in next 3 loops] 3 times, working in previously made ch-3 sps, [ch 1, sc in next ch 3 sp, ch 1, dc in each of next 3 loops] 3 times, [ch 1, sc in next ch 3 sp, ch 1, dc in next loop] twice**, [ch 3, dc in next loop] 8 times, rep from * around, ending last rep at **, [ch 3, dc in next loop] 3 times, ch 3, join in 3rd ch of beg ch-6.

Join the ends of the rib using the yarn ends of the rib and a crochet hook or tapestry needle. Insert the ends through the rib completing the rib pattern as much as possible. Fasten off on WS.

Rnd 2: Ch 4, sc in next ch-3 sp, *ch 3, dc in next ch-3 sp, ch 3, tr in next ch-3 sp, ch 3, tr in next ch-3 sp, ch 3, dc in next ch-3 sp**, [ch 3, sc in next ch-3 sp] 3 times, rep from * around, ending last rep at **, [ch 3, sc in next ch-3 sp] twice, ch 3, join in first ch of beg ch-4.

Rnd 3: Ch 1, 3 sc in each ch-3 sp, around, join in beg sc. Fasten off.

LOWER EDGE

On following rnd, dc loops tog, work all loops open.

Hold piece with Header at bottom, sk 3 loops from center bottom of any scallop, join in next loop, ch 5, dc in each of next 3 loops, [ch 3, dc in each of next 3 loops] twice, ch 3, [dc dec in next 3 loops] 4 times, working in previously made ch-3 sps, [ch 1, sc in next ch-3 sp, ch 1, dc in each of next 3 loops] 3 times, ch 1, sc in beg ch-5 sp, ch 3, sl st in next loop. Fasten off.

Rep for each rem scallop. ∎

Hairpin Lace Stole

DESIGN BY **TUSCA MARK**

SKILL LEVEL

INTERMEDIATE

FINISHED SIZE
23 x 66 inches

MATERIALS
- Lace weight mohair yarn:
  3½ oz/613 yds/100g color
  of choice
- Lace weight silk yarn:
  2 oz/350 yds/57g black
- Lace weight merino wool yarn:
  1 oz/175 yds/28g burgundy
- Size 7/1.65mm steel crochet hook
- Sizes D/3/3.25mm and F/5/3.75mm
  crochet hooks
- Tapestry needle
- Adjustable hairpin loom
- 4mm black seed beads: 388
- 6-inch square piece of cardboard

GAUGE
Gauge is not important for this item.

PATTERN NOTES
Loops twist naturally when removed from rods,
  do not untwist when working into them.

Join with slip stitch as indicated unless
  otherwise stated.

SPECIAL STITCH
Cluster (cl): Yo, insert hook in next ch sp, yo,
pull lp through, yo, pull through 2 lps on hook,
yo twice, insert hook in next ch sp, yo, pull lp
through, [yo, pull through 2 lps on hook] twice,
*yo 3 times, insert hook in next ch sp, yo, pull lp
through, [yo, pull through 2 lps on hook] 3 times,
rep from * once, yo twice, insert hook in next

ch sp, yo, pull lp through, [yo, pull through 2 lps on hook] twice, yo, insert hook in next ch sp, yo, pull lp through, yo, pull through 2 lps on hook, yo, pull through all lps on hook.

INSTRUCTIONS
SHAWL
STRIP
MAKE 6.

Remove top bar from loom. Adjust loom to 2½ inches. With mohair, make slip knot and place on left-hand rod of loom (see illustration 1), replace top bar. Pull yarn around right-hand side of loom to the back (see illustration 2). Insert hook into lp of slip knot and pull until knot is at center, yo, pull strand at back through lp on hook (see illustration 3), ch 1. *Drop lp from hook, insert hook in dropped lp from back to front, turn loom from right to left, passing the yarn

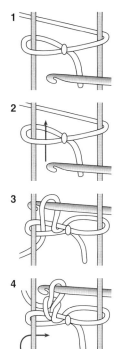

around to the back of the loom, yo, pull strand at back through lp on hook, insert hook under front strand of lp on left-hand side and pull yarn through, yo, pull through both lps on hook (see illustration 4), rep from * until 315 lps are on left-hand side and 316 lps are on right-hand side. If rods become too full, remove bottom bar and slip some lps off rods. At end of last lp, fasten off.

FIRST STRIP TOP EDGING
Row 1: Holding 1 Strip with 316-lp side at top, with size 7 hook and silk, join with sc in first lp, *[ch 3, sc in next lp] twice, [ch 3, insert hook through next 2 lps at same time, yo, pull lp through, complete as sc] twice, ch 3, insert hook through next 8 lps at same time, yo, pull lp through, complete as sc, [ch 3, insert hook

through next 2 lps at same time, yo, pull lp through, complete as sc] twice, [ch 3, sc in next lp] 3 times, rep from * 14 times, turn.

Row 2: Ch 4, *sc in next ch sp, ch 3, dc in next ch sp, ch 7, **cl** (see Special Stitch), ch 7, dc in next ch sp, ch 3, sc in next ch sp, rep from * 14 times, turn.

Row 3: Ch 1, 2 sc in first ch sp, 3 sc in each ch-3 sp and 7 sc in each ch-7 sp across to last ch sp, 2 sc in last sp. Fasten off.

FIRST STRIP BOTTOM EDGING
Holding First Strip with 315-lp side at top and size 7 hook and silk, holding first 4 lps tog as 1, join with sc in first 4 lps, *[ch 3, insert hook through next 2 lps at same time, yo, pull lp through, complete as sc] twice, [ch 3, sc in next lp] 5 times, [ch 3, insert hook through next 2 lps at same time, yo, pull lp through, complete as sc] twice**, ch 3, insert hook through next 8 lps at same time, yo, pull lp through, complete as sc, rep from * across, ending last rep at **, ch 3, insert hook in last 4 lps at same time, yo, pull lp through, complete as sc, ch 35. **Do not fasten off.**

2ND STRIP JOINING
Holding 315-lp side of next Strip and bottom edge of last Strip tog, insert hook in first 4 lps of new Strip at same time, yo, pull lp through, complete as sc, *[ch 3, insert hook through next 2 lps at same time, yo, pull lp through, complete as sc] twice, [ch 3, sc in next lp] twice, ch 1, sc in ch-3 sp between 2nd and 3rd single lps on other Strip, ch 1, sc in next lp on this Strip, ch 1, sc in ch-3 sp between 3rd and 4th single lps on other Strip, ch 1, sc in next lp on this Strip, ch 3, sc in next lp, [ch 3, insert hook in next 2 lps at same time, yo, pull lp through, complete as sc] twice**, ch 3, insert hook in next 8 lps at same time, yo, pull lp through, yo, complete as sc, rep from * across, ending last rep at **, ch 3, insert hook in last 4 lps at same time, yo, pull lp through, complete as sc, ch 35, sl st in end sc of last Strip. Fasten off.

2ND STRIP BOTTOM EDGING
Holding Strip with 316-lp side at top, with size 7 hook and silk, join with sc in first lp, *[ch 3, sc in next lp] twice, [ch 3, insert hook through next 2 lps at same time, yo, pull lp through,

complete as sc] twice, ch 3, insert hook through next 8 lps at same time, yo, pull lp through, complete as sc, [ch 3, insert hook through next 2 lps at same time, yo, pull lp through, complete as sc] twice, [ch 3, sc in next lp] 3 times, rep from * 14 times. Fasten off.

3RD STRIP JOINING

Holding 316-lp side of next Strip and bottom edge of last Strip tog, with size 7 hook and silk, join with sc in first lp of new Strip, ch 1, sc in ch-3 sp between first and 2nd single lps of last Strip, ch 1, sc in next lp on this Strip, *ch 3, sc in next lp, [ch 3, insert hook through next 2 lps at same time, yo, pull lp through, complete as sc] twice, ch 3, insert hook through next 8 lps at same time, yo, pull lp through, complete as sc, [ch 3, insert hook through next 2 lps at same time, yo, pull lp through, complete as sc] twice, [ch 3, sc in next lp] 2 times**, ch 1, sc in next ch-3 sp between 2nd and 3rd single lps on other Strip, ch 1, sc in next lp on this Strip, ch 1, sc in next ch-3 sp between 3rd and 4th single lps on other Strip, ch 1, dc in next lp on this Strip, rep from * across, ending last rep at **, ch 1, sc in ch sp between last 2 lps on other Strip, ch 1, sc in last lp on this Strip. Fasten off.

3RD STRIP BOTTOM EDGING
Work same as First Strip Bottom Edging.

4TH STRIP JOINING
Work same as 2nd Strip Joining.

4TH STRIP BOTTOM EDGING
Work same as 2nd Strip Bottom Edging.

5TH STRIP JOINING
Work same as 3rd Strip Joining.

5TH STRIP BOTTOM EDGING
Work same as 3rd Strip Bottom Edging.

6TH STRIP JOINING
Work same as 2nd Strip Joining.

6TH STRIP BOTTOM EDGING
Thread 136 beads onto silk, push beads back until needed.

Row 1: Holding Strip with 316 lp side at top, with size 7 hook and silk, join with sc in first lp, *[ch 3, sc in next lp] twice, [ch 3, insert hook through next 2 lps at same time, yo, pull lp through, complete as sc] twice, ch 3, insert hook through next 8 lps at same time, yo, pull lp through, complete as sc, [ch 3, insert hook through next 2 lps at same time, yo, pull lp through, complete as sc] twice, [ch 3, sc in next lp] 3 times, rep from * 14 times. Fasten off.

Row 2: Ch 2, pull up 1 bead, ch 3, sc in first ch-3 sp, *ch 3, pull up 1 bead, ch 3, sc in next ch-3 sp, rep from * across, ch 3, pull up 1 bead, ch 2, **join** (see Pattern Notes) in last st. Fasten off.

CENTER FILLER MOTIF

Rnd 1: Working in 1 diamond-shaped sp between Strips, with size D hook and wool, join in 2nd free ch-3 sp after joining, ch 6, dc in next ch-3 sp, ch 3, **dc dec** (see Stitch Guide) in next 2 ch sps, *[ch 3, dc in next ch-3 sp] twice, ch 3, dc dec in next 2 ch sps, rep from * around, ch 3, join in 3rd ch of beg ch-6.

Rnd 2: Sl st in next ch sp, ch 4, tr in each ch sp around, join in 4th ch of beg ch-4. Fasten off.

Work Filler Motif in each diamond-shaped opening between Strips.

SIDE FILLER MOTIF

Rnd 1: Working in 1 diamond-shaped sp formed by indentation on side edge of Shawl and ch-35 sp, with size D hook and wool, join in 2nd free ch-3 sp after joining, ch 6, dc in next ch-3 sp, ch 3, dc dec in next ch sp and 3rd ch of next ch-35, [ch 3, sk next 3 chs, dc in next ch] twice, ch 3, sk next 3 chs, dc dec in first and last of next 7 chs, [ch 3, sk next 3 chs, dc in next ch] twice, ch 3, sk next 3 chs, dc dec in next ch and next ch sp on Shawl, [ch 3, sc in next ch sp] twice, ch 3, dc dec in ch sps on each side of joining, ch 3, join in 3rd ch of beg ch-6.

Rnd 2: Sl st in next ch sp, ch 4, tr in each ch sp around, join in 4th ch of beg ch-4. Fasten off.

Work Side Filler Motif in each ch-35 sp on each side of Shawl.

TASSEL
MAKE 14.

For each Tassel, cut 3 strands silk each 12 inches in length, secure 6 beads randomly sp across each strand. Set aside.

Wrap silk around cardboard 45 times, slide off cardboard and cut lps at 1 end. Holding these and beaded strands tog, tie separate strand silk around center of strands. Fold strands in half, wrap another strand silk several times around strands ½ inch from fold, secure. Trim ends.

Tie 1 Tassel to each end of short edge and to end of each diamond section on each short end of Shawl. ■

Hairpin Lace Doily

DESIGN BY **MAGGIE PETSCH**

SKILL LEVEL

INTERMEDIATE

FINISHED SIZE
11 x 16½ inches

MATERIALS
- DMC Cebelia size 20 crochet cotton (50 grams per ball):
  1 ball each #799 horizon blue *(A)*, #800 sky blue *(B)* and #B5200 bright white *(C)*
- Size 9/1.25mm steel crochet hook or size needed to obtain gauge
- ⅞-inch hairpin frame
- Tapestry needle

GAUGE
Each Motif = 1¾ inches in diameter

PATTERN NOTES
Join rounds with slip stitch as indicated unless otherwise stated.

Always change colors in last stitch worked.

SPECIAL STITCHES
Shell: [2 dc, ch 3, 2 dc] in indicated st or ch sp.

Joining shell: [2 dc, ch 1] in indicated st or ch sp, sl st in ch sp of corresponding shell on previous Motif, ch 1, 2 dc in same ch sp on working Motif as last dc made.

Beginning shell (beg shell): (Ch 3, dc, ch 3, 2 dc) in indicated st or ch sp.

Beginning joining shell (beg joining shell): (Ch 3—*counts as first dc*, dc, ch 1) in indicated st on working Motif, sl st in ch sp of corresponding shell on previous Motif, ch 1, 2 dc in same st on working Motif as last dc made.

Joining chain-4 (joining ch-4): Ch 2, remove hook from lp, insert hook from RS to WS in corresponding ch-4 sp on previous Motif, pick up dropped lp, pull through ch-4 sp, ch 2.

Hairpin-stripe pattern: [Work 1 lp on each side with A, changing to B in sc on 2nd lp, work 1 lp on each side with B, changing to A in sc on 2nd lp] rep until desired number of lps have been completed on each side, **do not change** color after last lp has been worked. Fasten off.

Joined double crochet (joined dc): Dc dec *(see Stitch Guide)* in each of next 2 indicated ch sps.

INSTRUCTIONS
DOILY
HAIRPIN STRIP
MAKE 4 EACH WITH A AND B. MAKE 8 WITH A AND B
Make hairpin strip in **hairpin-stripe pattern** *(see Special Stitches)* with 1-sc spine and 36 loops on each side.

FIRST MOTIF
Rnd 1: Retaining twist in lps, **join** *(see Pattern Notes)* C through group of first 6 lps on either edge of any A hairpin strip, ch 1, sc in same sp, [**sc dec** *(see Stitch Guide)* in next 6 lps] around, join in beg sc. Fasten off. *(6 sc)*

With tapestry needle, tack ends of sc spine tog to form a ring.

Rnd 2: Retaining twist in lps, join C through group of any 2 lps on opposite edge of same hairpin strip, ch 1, sc in same sp, [ch 5, sc dec in next 2 lps] around, ending with ch 2, dc in beg sc to form last ch-5 sp. *(18 ch-5 sps)*

Rnd 3: **Beg shell** *(see Special Stitches)* in last ch sp just made, *ch 4, (sc, ch 3, sc, ch 4) in each of next 2 ch-5 sps**, **shell** *(see Special Stitches)* in center ch of next ch-5 sp, rep from * around,

ending last rep at **, join in 3rd ch of beg ch-3. Fasten off.

2ND MOTIF
Rnds 1 & 2: With any hairpin strip in A and B hairpin-stripe pattern, rep rnds 1 and 2 of First Motif.

Rnd 3 (joining rnd): Retaining twist in lps, join C through group of any 2 lps on outside edge of same hairpin strip, **beg joining shell** *(see Special Stitches)* in top of dc just made, joining ch-4 to next ch-4 sp on previous Motif, [(sc, ch 3, sc) in next ch-4 sp on working Motif, **joining ch-4** *(see Special Stitches)* to next ch-4 sp on previous Motif] twice, **joining shell** *(see Special Stitches)* in center ch of next ch-5 sp on working Motif *(1 side joined)*, continue around as for rnd 3 of First Motif.

REMAINING 13 MOTIFS

Rnds 1–3: Following joining diagram for color placement, rep rnds 1–3 of 2nd Motif, joining on as many sides as are indicated on joining diagram.

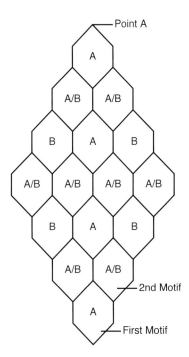

Hairpin Lace Doily
Joining Diagram

BORDER

Rnd 1: With RS facing, join A in ch sp of shell at right end of Doily *(Point A on joining diagram)*, ch 1, beg in same ch sp, ◊(sc, ch 5, sc) in ch sp of shell, *[ch 5, sc in next ch-4 sp] 3 times, ch 5, (sc, ch 5, sc) in ch sp of next shell, ch 5, [sc in next ch-4 sp, ch 5] 3 times, **joined dc** *(see Special Stitches)* in ch sps of next 2 shells, rep from * twice, **[ch 5, sc in next ch-4 sp] 3 times, ch 5, (sc, ch 5, sc) in ch sp of next shell, rep from ** once, [ch 5, sc in next ch-4 sp] 3 times, ch 5, joined dc in ch sp of next 2 shells, ***[ch 5, sc in next ch-4 sp] 3 times, ch 5, (sc, ch 5, sc) in ch sp of next shell, [ch 5, sc in next ch-4 sp] 3 times, ch 5, joined dc in ch sps of next 2 shells, rep from *** once, [ch 5, sc in next ch-4 sp] 3 times, ch 5, (sc, ch 5, sc) in next shell sp, ch 5, [sc in next ch-4 sp, ch 5] 3 times, rep from ◊ around, join in beg sc. Fasten off.

Rnd 2: With RS facing, join B in first ch-5 sp after joining st, beg shell in same ch sp, **ch 2, sc in next ch sp, *[ch 5, (sc, ch 3, sc) in next ch sp] twice, ch 5, sc in next ch sp, ch 2*, shell in next ch sp, ch 2, sc in next ch sp, rep between * once, shell in top of next joined dc, rep from ** twice, ch 2, sc in next ch sp, ch 5, [(sc, ch 3, sc) in next ch sp, ch 5] twice, sc in next ch sp, ch 2, shell in next ch sp, rep from ** once, ch 2, sc in next ch sp, [ch 5, (sc, ch 3, sc) in next ch sp] twice, ch 5, sc in next ch sp, ch 2***, shell in next sp, rep from ** around, ending last rep at ***, join in 3rd ch of beg ch-3. Fasten off.

Rnd 3: With RS facing, join C in ch sp of first shell after joining st, ch 1, (sc, ch 3, sc) in same ch sp, **[ch 5, (sc, ch 3, sc) in next ch-5 sp] 3 times, ch 5, (sc, ch 3, sc) in ch sp of next shell, *[ch 5, (sc, ch 3, sc) in next ch-5 sp] twice, ch 5, sc in next ch-5 sp, ch 5, sc in ch sp of next shell, ch 5, sc in next ch-5 sp, [ch 5, (sc, ch 3, sc) in next ch-5 sp] twice, ch 5, (sc, ch 3, sc) in ch sp of next shell, rep from * twice, rep from ** once, ch 5, [(sc, ch 3, sc) in next ch-5 sp, ch 5] 3 times***, [sc, ch 3, sc] in next shell sp, rep from ** around, ending last rep at ***, join in beg sc. Fasten off. ■

STITCH GUIDE

STITCH ABBREVIATIONS

beg . . . . begin/begins/beginning
bpdc . . . . back post double crochet
bpsc . . . . .back post single crochet
bptr . . . . .back post treble crochet
CC . . . . contrasting color
ch(s) . . . . chain(s)
ch- . . . . refers to chain or space
　　　　　　　　　 previously made (i.e., ch-1 space)
ch sp(s) . . . . chain space(s)
cl(s) . . . . cluster(s)
cm . . . . centimeter(s)
dc . . . . double crochet (singular/plural)
dc dec . . . . double crochet 2 or more
　　　　　　　　　　 stitches together, as indicated
dec . . . . decrease/decreases/decreasing
dtr . . . . double treble crochet
ext . . . . .extended
fpdc . . . . front post double crochet
fpsc . . . . front post single crochet
fptr . . . . front post treble crochet
g . . . . gram(s)
hdc . . . . half double crochet
hdc dec . . . . .half double crochet 2 or more
　　　　　　　　　　 stitches together, as indicated
inc . . . . increase/increases/increasing
lp(s) . . . . loop(s)
MC . . . . .main color
mm . . . . millimeter(s)
oz . . . . ounce(s)
pc . . . . popcorn(s)
rem . . . . remain/remains/remaining
rep(s) . . . . .repeat(s)
rnd(s) . . . . round(s)
RS . . . . right side
sc . . . . single crochet (singular/plural)
sc dec . . . . .single crochet 2 or more
　　　　　　　　　　 stitches together, as indicated
sk . . . . .skip/skipped/skipping
sl st(s) . . . . slip stitch(es)
sp(s) . . . . space(s)/spaced
st(s) . . . . stitch(es)
tog . . . . .together
tr . . . . treble crochet
trtr . . . . .triple treble
WS . . . . wrong side
yd(s) . . . . .yard(s)
yo . . . . yarn over

YARN CONVERSION

OUNCES TO GRAMS		GRAMS TO OUNCES	
1	28.4	25	7/8
2	56.7	40	1⅔
3	85.0	50	1¾
4	113.4	100	3½

UNITED STATES		UNITED KINGDOM
sl st (slip stitch)	=	sc (single crochet)
sc (single crochet)	=	dc (double crochet)
hdc (half double crochet)	=	htr (half treble crochet)
dc (double crochet)	=	tr (treble crochet)
tr (treble crochet)	=	dtr (double treble crochet)
dtr (double treble crochet)	=	ttr (triple treble crochet)
skip	=	miss

Single crochet decrease (sc dec):
(Insert hook, yo, draw lp through) in each of the sts indicated, yo, draw through all lps on hook.

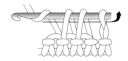

Example of 2-sc dec

Half double crochet decrease (hdc dec):
(Yo, insert hook, yo, draw lp through) in each of the sts indicated, yo, draw through all lps on hook.

Example of 2-hdc dec

Reverse Single Crochet (reverse sc):
Ch 1. Skip first st. [Working from left to right, insert hook in next st from front to back, draw up lp on hook, yo, and draw through both lps on hook.]

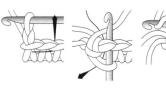

Chain (ch):
Yo, pull through lp on hook.

Single crochet (sc):
Insert hook in st, yo, pull through st, yo, pull through both lps on hook.

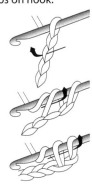

Double crochet (dc):
Yo, insert hook in st, yo, pull through st, [yo, pull through 2 lps] twice.

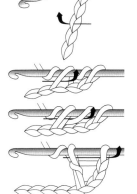

Double crochet decrease (dc dec):
Yo, insert hook, yo, draw loop through, draw through 2 lps on hook) in each of the sts indicated, yo, draw through all lps on hook.

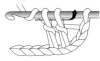

Example of 2-dc dec

Front loop (front lp) Back loop (back lp)
Front Loop　　Back Loop

Front post stitch (fp): Back post stitch (bp):
When working post st, insert hook from right to left around post st on previous row.

Back　Front

Post of Stitch

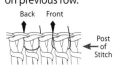

Half double crochet (hdc):
Yo, insert hook in st, yo, pull through st, yo, pull through all 3 lps on hook.

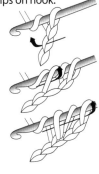

Double treble crochet (dtr):
Yo 3 times, insert hook in st, yo, pull through st, [yo, pull through 2 lps] 4 times.

Treble crochet decrease (tr dec):
Holding back last lp of each st, tr in each of the sts indicated, yo, pull through all lps on hook.

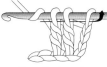

Example of 2-tr dec

Slip stitch (sl st):
Insert hook in st, pull through both lps on hook.

Chain Color Change (ch color change)
Yo with new color, draw through last lp on hook.

Double Crochet Color Change (dc color change)
Drop first color, yo with new color, draw through last 2 lps of st.

Treble crochet (tr):
Yo twice, insert hook in st, yo, pull through st, [yo, pull through 2 lps] 3 times.

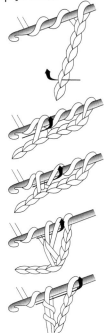

Metric Conversion Charts

METRIC CONVERSIONS

yards	x	.9144	=	metres (m)
yards	x	91.44	=	centimetres (cm)
inches	x	2.54	=	centimetres (cm)
inches	x	25.40	=	millimetres (mm)
inches	x	.0254	=	metres (m)

centimetres	x	.3937	=	inches
metres	x	1.0936	=	yards

INCHES INTO MILLIMETRES & CENTIMETRES (Rounded off slightly)

inches	mm	cm	inches	cm	inches	cm	inches	cm
1/8	3	0.3	5	12.5	21	53.5	38	96.5
1/4	6	0.6	5 1/2	14	22	56	39	99
3/8	10	1	6	15	23	58.5	40	101.5
1/2	13	1.3	7	18	24	61	41	104
5/8	15	1.5	8	20.5	25	63.5	42	106.5
3/4	20	2	9	23	26	66	43	109
7/8	22	2.2	10	25.5	27	68.5	44	112
1	25	2.5	11	28	28	71	45	114.5
1 1/4	32	3.2	12	30.5	29	73.5	46	117
1 1/2	38	3.8	13	33	30	76	47	119.5
1 3/4	45	4.5	14	35.5	31	79	48	122
2	50	5	15	38	32	81.5	49	124.5
2 1/2	65	6.5	16	40.5	33	84	50	127
3	75	7.5	17	43	34	86.5		
3 1/2	90	9	18	46	35	89		
4	100	10	19	48.5	36	91.5		
4 1/2	115	11.5	20	51	37	94		

KNITTING NEEDLES CONVERSION CHART

Canada/U.S.	0	1	2	3	4	5	6	7	8	9	10	10½	11	13	15
Metric (mm)	2	2¼	2¾	3¼	3½	3¾	4	4½	5	5½	6	6½	8	9	10

CROCHET HOOKS CONVERSION CHART

Canada/U.S.	1/B	2/C	3/D	4/E	5/F	6/G	8/H	9/I	10/J	10½/K	N
Metric (mm)	2.25	2.75	3.25	3.5	3.75	4.25	5	5.5	6	6.5	9.0

Annie's Attic®

Learn To Do Hairpin Lace is published by DRG, 306 East Parr Road, Berne, IN 46711.
Printed in USA. Copyright © 2010 DRG. All rights reserved. This publication may not be
reproduced in part or in whole without written permission from the publisher.

RETAIL STORES: If you would like to carry this pattern book or any other DRG publications, visit DRGwholesale.com

Every effort has been made to ensure that the instructions in this publication are complete
and accurate. We cannot, however, take responsibility for human error, typographical mistakes
or variations in individual work. Please visit AnniesCustomerCare.com to check for pattern updates.

ISBN: 978-1-59635-340-4